Basque Travel Guide 2025

Adventure, Food, and Outdoor Escapes from the Pyrenees to the Coast

Copyright

Preface

Every meal in the Basque Country is a celebration of flavor and workmanship, where rocky mountain trails meet golden beaches, and where centuries-old customs coexist with contemporary innovation. This unusual area, which is tucked away between Spain and France, has long been a secret treasure for travelers, foodies, and cultural explorers looking for something different.

This guide is an invitation to explore the Basque Country in all its richness, not just a book. This trip is yours to design, whether your desire is to hike the Pyrenees, surf the renowned waves of Biarritz, or indulge in the best pintxos in San Sebastián.

The Basque Country is a timeless destination that offers world-class cuisine, outdoor activities, and rich cultural traditions that make every visit special, even as travel continues to change in 2025. With professional insights, local suggestions, and well-chosen itineraries for all types of travelers, this book is made to make navigating the area easy.

I hope this book will encourage your travels, pique your interest, and allow you to discover the real essence of the Basque Country—a place that will stay with you long after you've left.

Table of Contents

Overview

Welcome to the Basque Country, a region known for its world-class cuisine, untamed coastlines, verdant mountains, and one of Europe's most distinctive cultures. The Basque Country, which lies between northern Spain and southwest France, is a place where modern innovation and ancient traditions coexist harmoniously and where every trip is a sensory extravaganza.

This area is where flavor and adventure collide. You might be hiking in the Pyrenees one minute, admiring the stunning vistas of misty peaks and undulating green hills. Next, you're enjoying a dish of pintxos, which are tiny, tasty morsels that are the Basque equivalent of tapas, or surfing the strong waves of the Bay of Biscay. The Basque Country offers a unique travel experience, regardless of your interests—adventure, cuisine, or just finding hidden treasures.

You will hear a language that sounds completely different from Spanish or French as you explore. That's Euskara, the Basque language, which is among the oldest and most enigmatic in the world. The fact that the Basques have maintained their independence, identity, and customs for centuries is evidence of their resilient nature.

Whether you're planning a leisurely getaway into nature, an intense exploration of Basque cuisine, or an action-packed outdoor activity, this guide is meant to help you get the most out of your trip.

Why Go in 2025?

The Basque Country is the ideal destination right now. In 2025, the area is teeming with fresh adventures, resurrected customs, and eco-friendly travel projects that enhance the pleasure of exploration.

This year is unique for the following reasons:

- A Vibrant Scene of Adventure
  Outdoor travel is becoming more and more popular. Both novice and expert hikers will find it easier to navigate the Pyrenees' hiking routes thanks to improved signage. More guided kayaking and paddleboarding tours are available than ever before, and surf schools around the coast, from Biarritz to Mundaka, are launching new

environmentally responsible programs.

- A Renaissance in Cooking
  Although Basque food has always been
  well-known throughout the world, 2025
  is bringing even more to the table. The
  greatest pintxos, seafood, and wines are
  being featured at local culinary festivals,
  and Michelin-starred restaurants in San
  Sebastián are introducing new tasting
  menus influenced by traditional Basque
  flavors. Additionally, historic customs
  are being revived by cider businesses,
  which offer tourists a real Basque
  drinking experience right out of the
  barrel.

- An Encouragement of Eco-Friendly
  Travel
  In terms of environmentally conscious
  travel, the Basque Country is setting the
  standard. Numerous trekking routes
  now incorporate "leave no trace"
  policies, and a number of isolated
  communities have embraced ecotourism
  by providing farm-to-table dining
  options and solar-powered eco-lodges.
  This is an exciting time for
  eco-conscious foodies to visit the Basque

Culinary Center because it is also encouraging zero-waste cooking.

- Unprecedented Festivals and Events
  2025 is jam-packed with cultural events that will never be forgotten, from the lively Semana Grande celebrations in Bilbao and San Sebastián to the San Fermín festival (Running of the Bulls) in Pamplona. Anticipate larger parades, more extensive music festivals, and significantly more tourist interaction.

2025 is the year to enjoy the best of the Basque Country, whether your goals are adventure, cuisine, or culture.

How to Utilize This Manual

This guide is intended to be your ideal traveling companion, facilitating your easy navigation of the Basque Country. From logistics and itineraries to in-depth explorations of regional customs, outdoor activities, and culinary experiences, it provides all you need to arrange your trip.

This is what you will discover:

- Organizing Your Trip – Travel necessities, budget advice, and the best times to go.
- Getting Around – How to find your way between towns, mountain paths, and coastal roads.
- Adventure Travel – The best places to hike, surf, and engage in exhilarating activities.
- Culinary Experiences – How to enjoy Basque cuisine like a local, where to dine, and what to try.
- Culture and History – An in-depth examination of the language, customs, and identity of the Basques.
- Sustainable Travel – Advice on how to assist small businesses while traveling in an ethical manner.
- Sample Itineraries – Pre-made arrangements for a variety of travel styles, whether you're visiting for a weekend getaway or an extended journey.

Everything you need to fully experience the charm of the Basque Country is included in this guide, whether you're using it to create a comprehensive schedule or just scan it for quick advice.

A Synopsis of Culture and History

With a history dating back thousands of years, the Basque Country is one of Europe's most mysterious areas. One of the oldest cultures in Europe is that of the Basques, or Euskaldunak, who inhabited this region long before Spain or France did.

The Basque language, Euskara, is unrelated to any other known tongue, in contrast to other European languages. For centuries, linguists and historians have been fascinated by this linguistic conundrum. The Basques are proud to still speak their own language in addition to Spanish and French.

The Basques have long been traders, seafarers, and fiercely independent individuals. They have maintained their own identity from the Middle Ages to the present despite a variety of obstacles, such as attempts to repress their culture by Spanish and French governments.

More than ever, Basque identity is honored today. With its own administration, customs, and educational system that supports Euskara, the area maintains a significant degree of autonomy.

Highlights of Culture:

- The Basque Sport Scene – The Basques are renowned for their distinctive traditional sports, such as herri kirolak (rural sports like stone lifting and wood chopping) and pelota (a fast-paced ball game).
- The Food Culture – Food plays a vital role in daily life, from San Sebastián's pintxos bars to Basque cider houses.
- Festivals and Folklore – Vibrant celebrations like Semana Grande and La Tamborrada (Drum Festival) highlight the area's passion for dance, music, and festivities.

As a visitor, you will sense the resilient, proud, and welcoming nature of the Basque people in every community, celebration, and cuisine sample.

Prepare for an Experience That Will Never Be Forgotten

The Basque Country offers a voyage full of exploration and adventure, whether your goals are to explore the Pyrenees, surf the Atlantic waves, or savor world-class food.

Prepare to discover one of the world's most fascinating locations by packing your bags and bringing your curiosity.

Making Travel Plans

The process of organizing a trip to the Basque Country is thrilling in and of itself. Knowing when to travel, how much to spend, and what to bring can make all the difference in this place with its varied landscapes, rich culinary heritage, and countless outdoor adventures. This area will help you get ready for a memorable trip, whether you're trekking in the Pyrenees, surfing along the coast, or enjoying world-class pintxos.

The Greatest Time to Go for Culinary and Outdoor Travel

The Basque Country offers year-round travel opportunities, which is one of its best features. However, the ideal time to visit will depend on your travel goals.

March-May: The Ideal Mix of Food and Adventure

Hikers and foodies alike will appreciate spring. With pleasant temperatures that are ideal for lengthy excursions, the hiking paths in the Pyrenees and along the coast are lush and colorful. The fresh fish season also begins in the spring, and many local eateries feature seasonal dishes on their menus. Additionally, it's a more sedate time to visit the cities before the busiest travel season arrives.

Summertime (June–August): Festivals and Outdoor Activities

The greatest time to go is in the summer if you like to surf, have beach activities, and attend exciting festivals. From San Sebastián to Biarritz, the coastline is teeming with activity, and surfers are enjoying the best waves. Additionally, this is the busiest time of year for cultural events, such as the Semana Grande celebration in San Sebastián and Bilbao, which features concerts, fireworks, and traditional Basque acts.

But remember that summer is also the busiest time of year, particularly in major cities. Choose less crowded beaches along the Basque coast or travel into the highlands for a more sedate getaway.

Fall (September–November): Cider, Wine, and Fewer Crowds

One of the best seasons to travel to the Basque Country is in the fall. The weather is still nice, but the summer crowds have vanished. Since it's harvest season, now is the ideal time to visit the vineyards of Rioja Alavesa or take in the bustling traditional Basque cider houses. The autumnal hues of the Basque countryside's trees and the lower temperatures will appeal to hikers.

Winter (December–February): Highlights of Surfing and Cozy Retreats

Explore the medieval towns, quaint cider houses, and indoor food markets during the peaceful and charming winter months in the Basque Country. Surfing is at its height, with strong swells drawing experienced surfers from all over the world, while high-altitude hiking paths could be blanketed in snow. Winter is a terrific time of year if you want a quiet vacation with amazing meals and fewer tourists.

Costs and Budgeting

From Michelin-starred restaurants to reasonably priced local taverns, and from luxurious resorts to guesthouses, the Basque Country has travel experiences to suit every budget. Here's a broad breakdown of what you should expect in terms of costs:

Costs of Accommodation

- Budget (€30–€60 per night): Hostels, small guesthouses, and budget hotels. Campsites are also an affordable option for outdoor explorers.
- Mid-range (€70–€150 per night): Boutique hotels, charming rural accommodations, and comfortable city stays.
- Luxury (€200+ per night): High-end hotels, opulent lodges, and paradores (historic hotels in castles or monasteries).

Costs of Food and Dining

- Budget (€10–€20 per meal): Affordable pintxos in bakeries, bars, and casual eateries.
- Mid-range (€25–€50 per meal): A full meal at a traditional Basque restaurant or cider house.
- Luxury (€100+ per meal): Gourmet tasting menus, wine pairings, and Michelin-starred dining.

Costs of Adventure and Activities

- Free: Walking around Basque towns, hiking, and self-guided beach walks.

- Mid-range (€30–€80): Wine tastings, guided hikes, and surfboard rentals.
- Luxury (€100+): Exclusive wine and food tours, hot air balloon rides, or private surfing lessons.

While budget travelers can explore the Basque Country for about €50 to €70 per day, a typical mid-range traveler should budget €100 to €150 per day.

Important Travel Advice

1. Acquire a Few Basque Expressions
   Locals value guests who know a few words of Euskara (the Basque language), even though Spanish and French are the most commonly spoken languages. Try:

   - Kaixo! – Hi there!
   - Eskerrik asko! – Thank you!
   - Bai/Ez – Yes/No
2. Embrace the Local Dining Culture

   - Pintxos are self-serve at Basque bars, but you pay based on what you consume.
   - Join in on the popular local tradition of txikiteo (bar-hopping).

- Cider houses often offer family-style meals with unlimited cider.
3. Use Public Transportation or Rent a Car for Rural Exploration

    - Cities like San Sebastián and Bilbao have excellent public transportation.
    - Renting a car is highly recommended for exploring the mountains and rural villages.
4. Respect Traditions and the Environment

    - Stick to designated trails when hiking to protect the ecosystem.
    - Support small, local businesses for an authentic Basque experience.

Adventure and Food Lovers' Packing Guide

The season and the activities you have planned will determine how you should pack for the Basque Country. Here's a checklist to help you prepare.

For Outdoor Adventures

- Hiking boots: Essential for rugged coastal walks and Pyrenean trails.
- Layers and quick-dry clothing: The weather can change rapidly, especially in the mountains.
- Rain jacket: Rainfall is common, particularly in spring and fall.
- Backpack: Ideal for carrying essentials on day trips.
- Swimwear: Perfect for coastal surfing and beach days.
- Sunscreen and sunglasses: The sun can be intense even on cloudy days.

For Food and Culture Travel

- Smart-casual attire: Many restaurants have a relaxed yet stylish dress code.
- Comfortable shoes: Essential for walking in villages with cobblestone streets.
- Reusable water bottle: Many towns have public fountains with drinkable water.
- Notebook or food journal: Record your favorite wines and pintxos!

Additional Travel Essentials

- Power adapter: The Basque Country uses European Type C and F plugs.
- Cash and card: Many small bars and rural shops prefer cash payments.
- eSIM or local SIM card: Useful for reliable mobile data while traveling.

The Basque Country is a dream destination for both food lovers and outdoor enthusiasts, offering stunning landscapes, exceptional cuisine, and rich cultural traditions. By planning ahead, you can maximize your adventure and ensure a stress-free, unforgettable experience. Pack your bags, bring your appetite, and get ready to explore one of Europe's most vibrant and culturally rich regions!

Traveling to the Basque

Whether you're coming from Spain, France, or elsewhere, the Basque Country is easily accessible by air, train, or road thanks to its excellent connections. Getting about the region is as interesting as the destination itself because of cross-border connections, gorgeous driving routes, and effective public transportation. This chapter covers the best routes to get to the Basque Country and how to get around once you're there.

Traveling by Road, Train, and Air

By Air: Basque Country Airports

Flying is frequently the most practical option for visitors from other countries to get to the Basque Country. With direct flights from major European cities and beyond, the area is served by several airports.

- Bilbao Airport (BIO) – The biggest and busiest airport in the Basque Country, providing excellent connections to Spain's major cities and international flights. Located just 12 kilometers from

Bilbao, it is an ideal option for those traveling to San Sebastián, Bilbao, or the Rioja Alavesa wine region.

- San Sebastián Airport (EAS) – A small airport offering limited but useful domestic flights, mainly connecting via Madrid and Barcelona. It is perfect for those exploring the eastern coast of the Basque Country.
- Biarritz Pays Basque Airport (BIQ) – Situated just across the border in France, this airport is an excellent alternative for those visiting San Sebastián or the French Basque coast. It provides flights from various European cities, including Paris and London.
- Vitoria Airport (VIT) – A quieter airport, primarily handling seasonal and low-cost flights. It is a convenient choice for visitors heading to Rioja Alavesa and the Basque hinterlands.

By Train: Regional and High-Speed Rail Links

Train travel is a pleasant and scenic option, thanks to the excellent rail connections to the Basque Country offered by France's SNCF and Spain's Renfe train networks.

- From Madrid – The Renfe Alvia high-speed train takes approximately five hours to reach Bilbao and San Sebastián.
- From Barcelona – The train ride to Bilbao or San Sebastián takes about six hours.
- From France – The SNCF high-speed TGV takes around four hours to travel from Paris to Hendaye (on the French border). From there, a transfer to Euskotren regional trains takes just 40 minutes to reach San Sebastián.

Getting to the Basque Country by Road

The Basque Country is easily accessible by car for those who enjoy flexible travel schedules and road trips. The region is connected to major cities in France and Spain by a well-maintained highway network.

- From Madrid – A four-hour drive via the A-1 highway.
- From Barcelona – A 5.5-hour drive via the AP-2 and AP-68 highways.
- From Bordeaux, France – A 2.5-hour drive south on the A63 highway.

When renting a car, keep in mind:

- National roads (A roads) are usually free, while some freeways (AP roads) have tolls.

Regional Transportation Advice

The Basque Country's pedestrian-friendly cities, picturesque drives, and efficient public transportation make getting around simple once you arrive.

Public Transportation: Buses and Trains

- Euskotren (Basque Train Network) – The best option for travel between San Sebastián, Bilbao, and the French border. Trains are affordable, reliable, and clean.
- Renfe Cercanías (Commuter Trains) – Connects Bilbao to nearby towns and villages.
- Intercity Buses – Comfortable coach services between Basque cities and smaller towns are provided by companies such as ALSA and PESA.

Navigating Urban Areas

- Bilbao Metro – One of Spain's most modern metro systems, ideal for exploring Bilbao and surrounding areas.
- Trams – Available in Vitoria and San Sebastián, offering a convenient way to navigate city centers.
- City Buses – Each major Basque city has a reliable bus system. In San Sebastián, the D-Bus system is the most efficient way to get around.

Renting a Car and Driving

For exploring the Basque countryside, wine regions, and remote coastal towns, renting a car is the best option. However, parking in cities can be expensive and limited. If you plan to rent a car:

- Use park-and-ride facilities outside major cities.
- Be aware that historic centers often have narrow streets.
- Consider renting a small car for easier parking and navigation.

Walking and Cycling

With designated bike lanes in places like San Sebastián, the Basque Country is a bike-friendly destination. Walking and cycling are excellent ways to explore at a leisurely pace, and many coastal and rural routes are ideal for these activities.

International Travel: France and Spain

One of the unique advantages of traveling to the Basque Country is the seamless transition between Spain and France. Crossing the border is simple, and the region retains a strong cultural identity.

Bus and Train Service Between France and Spain

- Euskotren's "Topo" Line – This convenient train takes just 40 minutes to travel between San Sebastián, Spain, and Hendaye, France. From Hendaye, travelers can board the SNCF TGV to Bordeaux and Biarritz.
- Buses to Biarritz and Bayonne – Several companies, including ALSA and FlixBus, operate daily services between San Sebastián and French Basque cities.

Traveling by Car from Spain to France

Driving between the Spanish and French Basque regions is straightforward, with multiple road crossings.

- The A63 highway is the fastest route to Biarritz.
- Smaller border roads offer scenic drives through traditional Basque villages.

When driving between the two countries, keep in mind:

- No border controls – France and Spain are both in the Schengen Zone.
- Different road signs and speed limits – While both countries use km/h, France has different signage than Spain.
- Fuel prices – Gasoline is often cheaper in Spain than in France, so it's worth checking prices before refueling.

Crossing the Border on Foot and Bicycle

For adventurous travelers, walking or cycling across the border provides a unique experience. Popular routes include:

- Camino de Santiago – A historic pilgrimage route that passes through the Basque Country.
- Basque Coast Trail – A breathtaking coastal path from Hendaye, France, to Hondarribia, Spain.

Traveling to the Basque Country is easy and rewarding, whether by car, train, or plane. Once there, the region offers convenient cross-border travel, scenic drives, and efficient public transportation. No matter how you choose to explore, you'll quickly immerse yourself in the Basque Country's rich culture, stunning landscapes, and exceptional cuisine. Now that you know how to get here, it's time to start planning your adventure!

Getting Around the Basque

Getting around the Basque Country is part of the adventure once you're there. Traveling between towns and into the countryside is made easy and pleasurable by well-maintained highways, picturesque train routes, and contemporary public transportation. This chapter will make it easy for you to get around the area whether you decide to use the train, rent a car, or explore on two wheels.

Public Transportation: Trains, Buses, and Bicycles

For tourists who would rather not drive, public transportation in the Basque Country is an excellent choice because it is reasonably priced, dependable, and well-connected.

Trains: A Beautiful and Effective Way to Travel

With two major train operators, the Basque Country boasts a first-rate rail network:

- The Basque regional train system, Euskotren, is ideal for getting from one city to another and between small communities. Along a picturesque seaside path, it links Bilbao, San Sebastián, and Hendaye (France).

- Spain's national rail network, Renfe, provides regional and high-speed trains between the Basque Country and major cities including Barcelona, Madrid, and Zaragoza.

Euskotren is a great choice for day visits because it provides regular services and beautiful views of the countryside and coast.

Buses: An Affordable and Vast Network

Buses are frequently the most convenient mode of transportation if your plan includes stops in smaller towns. Numerous businesses are active in the area:

- PESA and ALSA connect major Basque cities regionally and over large distances.
- The greatest means of transportation within cities are D-Bus (San Sebastián) and Bilbobus (Bilbao).
- La Burundesa provides a practical way to get to national parks and rural areas.

Buses are a fantastic option for tourists on a tight budget because they are dependable and reasonably priced, and their routes go through practically every area of the Basque Country.

Biking: An Eco-Friendly and Enjoyable Way to Travel

The Basque Country is a great place to go riding if you like active vacations. The Basque Coast and Pyrenees offer amazing cycling routes, and cities like San Sebastián and Vitoria-Gasteiz have bike lanes and rental services.

- San Sebastián's Bidegorris is a system of beautiful bike routes that links the city's top locations.
- Bilbao's Bilbaobizi offers a fantastic bike-sharing program for quick excursions.
- The Basque Coast Bike Route runs from Bilbao to Biarritz, making it a breathtaking option for long-distance riders.

An enjoyable, eco-friendly, and engaging method to see the area at your own speed is by bicycle.

Car Rental vs. Public Transportation

Is Renting a Car Necessary?

You may travel freely and adaptably when you rent a car, particularly if you want to see the mountains, the Basque countryside, and undiscovered coastal towns. An automobile is especially helpful if you wish to:

- Explore isolated locations such as the Rioja Alavesa wine region or Gorbeia Natural Park.
- Take picturesque road trips into the Pyrenees or along the Basque Coast.
- Take your time exploring, making stops at overlooks, remote fishing ports, and neighborhood cider houses.

However, there are certain difficulties when driving in the Basque Country:

- Parking is costly and scarce in places like San Sebastián and Bilbao.
- Traveling on toll roads (AP highways) may result in additional expenses.
- Certain rural roads are twisty and narrow, necessitating strong driving abilities.

When Using Public Transportation Is Better

Public transportation is a preferable option for people who choose to stay in large cities and towns. You won't require a vehicle if:

- Public transportation is effective in the cities where you are staying, such as Vitoria-Gasteiz, San Sebastián, or Bilbao.
- You would rather travel without stress and without having to worry about parking or gas prices.
- Buses and trains service the metropolitan and seaside areas that are the center of your journey.

Consider taking public transportation most of the time and hiring a car exclusively for day trips if you want a little bit of both.

Language Advice: French, Spanish, and Euskara

The linguistic diversity of the Basque Country is among its most distinctive features. Spanish and Euskara (Basque) are the two official languages of the territory, while French is also often spoken in the north.

Euskara: The Basques' Language

Unrelated to any other language, Euskara is among the oldest in Europe. Euskara is a vital component of Basque identity, even though the majority of residents also speak Spanish (or French in the French Basque Country).

Although you don't have to speak Euskara to get around, knowing a few phrases can improve your experience and show respect. You'll discover bilingual signs everywhere.

Basic Phrases in Euskara

- Kaixo – Hi
- Eskerrik Asko – Thank you
- Agur – Goodbye
- Mesedez – Please
- Bai/Ez – Yes/No

You'll probably receive a friendly greeting if you use Kaixo to meet a local!

In the Basque Country, Spanish

The primary language in Bilbao, San Sebastián, and other cities is Spanish, which is also widely spoken. You won't have any problems getting about the area if you speak Spanish.

Practical Phrases in Spanish

- Hola, ¿cómo estás? – Hello, how are you?
- ¿Dónde está la estación de tren? – Where is the train station?
- Por favor, un café. – Please buy me a coffee.

The Northern Basque Country's French

Although Euskara is still spoken, French is the most common language in the French Basque Country (Pays Basque). It can be useful to know a little bit of French if you intend to travel to Biarritz, Bayonne, or Saint-Jean-de-Luz.

Typical Phrases in French

- Bonjour – Hello
- Merci – Thank you
- Où est la gare? – Where is the train station?

Language barriers are rarely a problem because the majority of employees in lodging facilities, dining establishments, and tourist destinations speak English, Spanish, or French.

Navigating the Basque Country is simple and part of the experience, whether you choose to go by bus, train, car, or bicycle. While renting a car allows access to more distant locations, public transportation is effective and reasonably priced. You can also enhance your experience and establish a connection with the local culture by learning a few Euskara, Spanish, and French phrases. The breathtaking scenery, rich traditions, and hospitable people of the Basque Country make any trip worthwhile, regardless of how you decide to travel.

Outdoor Activities

Climbing, Hiking, and Other Activities

With a scenery that skillfully combines rocky mountains, striking cliffs, undulating green hills, and picturesque seaside pathways, the Basque Country is an outdoor lover's dream. There are several adventure options in the Pyrenees, whether you're a seasoned hiker looking for high-altitude paths, a rock climber attracted to the area's limestone crags, or a tourist taking leisurely strolls through quaint Basque communities.

To guarantee that you see the untamed and magnificent side of the Basque Country, this chapter will lead you through the top hiking routes, climbing locations, and picturesque strolling paths.

Top Hiking Paths Along the Coast and in the Pyrenees

Hikes in the Pyrenees: Magnificent Peaks and Alpine Beauty

Some of the most difficult and rewarding hikes in the Basque Country can be found in the Pyrenees, which naturally divide Spain and France. Along the trip, you can see chamois, eagles, and wild horses as you go past high-altitude lakes, beautiful valleys, and magnificent hills.

Gorbeia Natural Park (the 1,481-meter-high Mount Gorbea)

- Why visit? Mount Gorbea, the highest summit in the Basque Country, has expansive views that extend to the Bay of Biscay.
- Trail length: Moderate to difficult, 12–15 km
- Highlights: A picturesque climb that passes through open meadows, limestone formations, and beech woodlands before arriving at the famous cross at the top.

Aizkorri-Aratz Natural Park (1,528-meter-high Aizkorri Peak)

- Why visit? With its rocky limestone peaks and subterranean caverns, this is the tallest mountain range in the Basque Country.

- Trail length: Tough, 10–14 km
- Highlights: The opportunity to witness the spiritual Camino de Santiago path going through the region, breathtaking rocky scenery, and mountain refuges.

Hikes Along the Coast: Ocean Views and Cliffside Paths

The Basque Coast has some of Europe's most breathtaking cliffside treks for individuals who enjoy sea breezes and striking coastal scenery. These paths meander around the rocky coastline, past beautiful rock formations, charming fishing communities, and secret coves.

Flysch Road (Deba to Zumaia)

- Why visit? With breathtaking Flysch rock formations rising over the ocean, this journey transports you through millions of years of geological history.
- Trail length: Moderate, 14 km
- Highlights: Little beaches, incredible rock strata formations, and *Game of Thrones* filming sites.

Trail of San Juan de Gaztelugatxe

- Why visit? A quick yet famous climb that connects a dramatic islet with a medieval hermitage across a meandering stone bridge.
- Trail length: Moderate, 3 km
- Highlights: Sweeping views of the coast, a stone staircase with 241 steps, and the myth that you can make a wish if you ring the church bell three times.

The paths in the Basque Country provide breathtaking views and life-changing outdoor experiences, regardless of your preference for the coast or the mountains.

Adventures in Rock Climbing and Caving

Climbing Rocks: Overcome the Basque Mountains

With limestone cliffs, bouldering routes, and multi-pitch climbs for all skill levels, the Basque Country is a top climbing destination. There is something for everyone, whether you are an experienced climber looking for a challenge or a novice looking for an introduction to the sport.

Atxarte (Durango)

- Why visit? With more than 400 routes on limestone cliffs, this is one of the most well-known climbing locations in the Basque Country.
- Ideal for: Climbers who are intermediate to experienced.
- Highlights: Multi-pitch routes, stunning vertical cliffs, and a lovely location in Urkiola Natural Park.

Etxauri (Near Pamplona)

- Why visit? Known for its varied routes and stunning landscape, this is one of the top sport climbing destinations in northern Spain.
- Ideal for: Novice to experienced climbers.
- Highlights: More than 700 climbs, routes that face various directions allowing for year-round climbing, and breathtaking views of the valley.

For those who are new to climbing, the area's climbing schools and guided tours provide professional instruction and equipment rentals to help you get started safely.

Caving: Investigating the Underground Environment

A secret world of caverns, underground rivers, and prehistoric rock formations can be found beneath the Basque terrain. Whether you're exploring deep underground chambers or touring prehistoric caves decorated with old art, caving in the area is an exciting activity.

Pozalagua Cave

- Why visit? Renowned for possessing the world's biggest collection of bizarre stalactites, which create an unearthly underworld scene.
- Ideal for: Vacationers and families.
- Highlights: Guided tours that highlight unique rock formations and stunning tunnels.

Arrikrutz Cave (Oñati)

- Why visit? Features fossils, an extensive network of underground caverns, underground rivers, and an intriguing past of animal and human life.
- Ideal for: History and geology-minded adventurers.

- Highlights: An exhilarating guided caving trip, prehistoric cave bear fossils, and hidden underground lakes.

Caving in the Basque Country is a once-in-a-lifetime experience for everyone looking for a distinctive and exhilarating adventure.

Beautiful Strolls Through Basque Towns

The quaint villages of the Basque Country provide lovely walking routes that lead you through classic streets, traditional farmhouses, and stunning rural vistas if you're looking for a more laid-back and immersive outdoor experience.

The Old Town Walk of Hondarribia

- Why visit? A delightful walk through one of the most picturesque coastal villages, featuring a gorgeous harbor, cobbled alleys, and colorful Basque homes.
- Trail length: Easy, 3–5 km
- Highlights: Views of the French coast, lively pintxos bars, and medieval city walls.

Walk Along the Coast from Elantxobe to Mundaka

- Why visit? A picturesque stroll through a fishing community that passes by wooded trails, rocks, and expansive vistas.
- Trail length: Moderate, 6 km
- Highlights: Picturesque harbors, the culture of Basque fishermen, and a breathtaking conclusion in Mundaka, a well-known surf town.

These hikes provide a slower but incredibly fulfilling way to see the Basque Country for those who are interested in culture, history, and the outdoors.

The Basque Country is an outdoor adventurer's paradise, offering everything from strenuous climbs in the Pyrenees to stunning coastline paths, world-class rock climbing, exhilarating caving trips, and picturesque village walks.

Every step you take here will be an amazing voyage through some of Europe's most breathtaking landscapes, whether you're seeking tranquil country walks or high-adrenaline activities.

Coastal Adventures

Water Sports, and Surfing

The Basque Country is a haven for lovers of water sports, with its untamed Atlantic surf, golden beaches, and striking cliffs. The Basque coast provides countless water sports, whether you're sailing along the rocky shoreline, kayaking or paddle boarding across the water, or surfing world-class waves at Biarritz and San Sebastián.

This chapter examines the best ways to enjoy the breathtaking waters of the Bay of Biscay, from the exhilarating thrill of big-wave surfing to the tranquil beauty of secret coves that are only reachable by boat.

The Best Places to Surf in San Sebastián and Biarritz

Some of Europe's top surf spots can be found in the Basque Country, which attracts both experienced surfers and those just starting out. It's hardly surprising that the area has been a surfing mecca for decades due to its famed surf culture, sandy beaches, and steady swells.

San Sebastián: The Best of Urban Surfing

In addition to being well-known for its cuisine, culture, and architecture, San Sebastián is a surfing destination with conveniently accessible waves in the heart of the city.

- Beach at Zurriola
    - Ideal for: Novice to experienced surfers
    - Why visit? This bustling beach has a thriving local scene, surf schools, and reliable waves.
    - Highlights: Take a lesson, rent a board, then visit the neighboring Old Town for cider and pintxos to cap off the day.

The Origin of European Surfing at Biarritz

Biarritz is regarded as Europe's first surfing hotspot and is located in French Basque Country, just across the border. It's a must-see for any surfer because of its chic atmosphere and flawless waves.

- The Basques Islands

    - Ideal for: Novice and experienced surfers

- - Why visit? With breathtaking vistas of the Pyrenees, this is a classic surf site where the sport first gained popularity in Europe.
  - Highlights: An iconic surf town ambiance, lots of surf schools, and smooth, rolling waves.
- The Grande Plage

  - Ideal for: Skilled surfers
  - Why visit? With strong waves and a vibrant beachside environment, this is one of France's most well-known surfing beaches.
  - Highlights: A traditional European beach town atmosphere, fast, hollow waves, and opulent hotels with views of the surf.

Mundaka: The Best Left-Hand Barrel in Europe

- Ideal for: Skilled surfers
- Why visit? This tiny fishing community is well-known throughout the world for having one of Europe's top left-hand waves, which is flawless and powerful.

- Highlights: A deep-rooted Basque surf tradition, a breathtaking river-mouth backdrop, and long, strong rides.

Local surf schools make it simple for beginners to start surfing and enjoy the rush of riding the Atlantic waves by providing lessons and rentals.

Bay of Biscay Kayaking and Stand-Up Paddleboarding

Kayaking and stand-up paddleboarding (SUP) are great alternatives to surfing if you'd rather explore the Basque coastline in a more sedate manner. Explore secret beaches at your own speed, kayak through sea caverns, or glide across turquoise waves.

- La Concha Bay (San Sebastián) Paddleboarding

    - Ideal for: Novice and recreational paddlers
    - Why visit? La Concha Bay is the ideal location for stand-up paddleboarding because of its serene, pristine seas.
    - Highlights: Explore Santa Clara Island, paddle by the classy

promenade, and take in a serene seaside vista of the city.

- Kayaking in the Biosphere Reserve of Urdaibai

  - Ideal for: Adventurers and nature enthusiasts
  - Why visit? This UNESCO-protected estuary is ideal for kayaking since it has mangroves, animals, and breathtaking river scenery.
  - Highlights: Explore the verdant surrounds, paddle through serene waters, and see herons and ospreys.

Kayaking through Sea Caves and Cliffs

Rent a kayak and paddle along the rocky cliffs of the Basque coastline for a more dramatic coastal experience. There, you'll discover secret caverns, arches, and remote beaches.

- Gaztelugatxe, San Juan
  - Ideal for: Kayakers with some experience
  - Why visit? For a distinctive view of its stone bridge and cliffside church, approach this gorgeous

islet—which was prominently featured in *Game of Thrones*—from the water.

- Highlights: Discover sea caverns, paddle beneath imposing rock formations, and land on undiscovered beaches that are unreachable by foot.

Experience the natural splendor of the Basque Country in a leisurely yet daring style with kayaking and SUP, whether you're paddling along the coast or gliding through serene estuaries.

Boat Tours and Sailing on the Basque Coast

Take a coastal tour or sailing boat for a more relaxed way to see the Basque waterways. The Bay of Biscay can be explored by boat in a variety of ways, from sunset sails to deep-sea fishing excursions.

- Getxo (near Bilbao) Sailing Tours

    - Ideal for: Unwinding and admiring breathtaking views of the ocean

- Why visit? Beautiful views of the Basque coastline, including Bilbao's harbor, rocky cliffs, and undiscovered beaches, may be seen from Getxo on a sailing excursion.
- Highlights: See dolphins, sip on a glass of local wine, and watch the sunset over the Atlantic.
- Observing Whales and Dolphins in San Sebastián and Bermeo

    - Ideal for: Those who love wildlife
    - Why visit? Whales, dolphins, and occasionally even orcas can be seen in the deep waters of the Bay of Biscay.
    - Highlights: See dolphin pods, discover local marine life, and enjoy a boat ride across the wide-open ocean.
- Charters for Fishing in the Bay of Biscay

    - Ideal for: Those looking for a local experience and those who enjoy fishing
    - Why visit? Take a traditional boat ride with Basque fishermen to get

a personal look at one of the oldest customs in the area.

- ○ Highlights: Savor the freshest seafood on the boat while trying your hand at catching sea bass, tuna, or mackerel.

A boat excursion is an incredibly unique opportunity to experience the Basque Country from a different angle, whether you're sailing along the coastline, seeing wildlife, or enjoying the excitement of deep-sea fishing.

The Basque Country provides a remarkable variety of coastal experiences, from kayaking to discovering secret beaches or sailing along the breathtaking coastline to surfing some of Europe's best waves. The waters of the Bay of Biscay encourage you to plunge in and explore, whether you're a seasoned surfer searching for the ideal break, a novice seeking a serene paddleboarding location, or a tourist hoping to unwind on a boat tour.

Outdoor Stays & Camping

Camping in the Basque Country is an experience that will never be forgotten, whether you want to sleep under a blanket of stars in a secluded valley, watch the sunrise over the Pyrenees, or wake up to the sound of waves crashing on the Bay of Biscay. The area provides a variety of outdoor lodging options that will let you get closer to nature, whether your preference is for distinctive eco-lodges, remote mountain retreats, or coastal campsites.

This chapter examines the top locations for sleeping beneath the stars, getting back in touch with nature, and taking in the stunning scenery of the area, from primitive cabins in the middle of the Basque woodlands to surfside camping in Biarritz.

Top Campsites in Coastal and Mountain Regions

Because of the Basque Country's varied geography, you may set up your tent or park your campervan in a variety of breathtaking locations, including high-altitude meadows, verdant valleys, and coastal cliffs. The following are a few of the top campgrounds for an engaging outdoor experience:

Camping Along the Sea: A Place to Sleep

These beachside campgrounds are ideal if you enjoy seeing the ocean when you get up and listening to the waves as you go to sleep.

- Playa de Zarautz Camp (Spain)

  - Ideal for: Surfers and beach lovers
  - Why stay? This campsite, perched on a cliffside with a view of Zarautz Beach, provides easy access to world-class surf and a vibrant town vibe.
  - Highlights: Nearby pintxos bars, convenient beach access, and breathtaking sunsets.
- Ilbarritz Camping (France, close to Biarritz)

  - Ideal for: Families and individuals looking for a blend of urban and natural life

- Why stay? This campground offers both leisure and adventure, and it's only a short drive from Biarritz's surf beaches and quaint old town.
- Highlights: A family-friendly environment, contemporary amenities, and a beach within walking distance.

Sleeping Amidst the Peaks at Mountain Campsites

The rocky peaks and undulating hills of the Basque Country offer a memorable camping experience for people who enjoy the peace and quiet of the highlands.

- Urrobi Camping (Navarre, Spain, close to the Pyrenees)

  - Ideal for: Nature enthusiasts and hikers
  - Why stay? This campsite, surrounded by rivers and lush woodlands, serves as a starting point for Pyrenean hiking paths.
  - Highlights: Nearby waterfalls, superb stargazing, and the

opportunity to see wildlife such as eagles and deer.

- Grotte de Sare Camping (France, close to the Basque mountains)

  - Ideal for: Cave explorers and adventurers
  - Why stay? This location, which is close to the Sare Caves, is ideal for trekking green hills, discovering underground treasures, and taking in Basque country life.
  - Highlights: Close proximity to traditional Basque communities, stunning mountain views, and unique cave trips.

Distinct Outdoor Experiences: Cabins, Eco-Lodges, and Rural Getaways

The Basque Country has eco-friendly lodges, quaint cabins, and classic rural retreats that combine sustainability and nature for tourists seeking an outdoor experience with extra comfort.

Glamping and Eco-Lodges: Sustainable Outdoor Accommodations

These eco-lodges and glamping locations provide the ideal balance of luxury and adventure for those who enjoy the outdoors but would rather sleep in a comfortable bed than a sleeping bag.

- The Ecology of the Basque Country (France)

  - Ideal for: Eco-aware tourists
  - Why stay? These lodges, tucked away in the Basque countryside, were constructed with renewable energy and sustainable materials.
  - Highlights: Solar-powered cabins, organic farm-to-table food, and activities that emphasize the environment.
- Suites at Basoa (Navarre, Spain)

  - Ideal for: Couples and travelers looking for a distinctive woodland experience
  - Why stay? For a dreamlike experience in the middle of the forest, stay in treehouse cabins hung amid the trees.
  - Highlights: Eco-friendly design, expansive treetop vistas, and a private setting.

Rural Getaways: Customary Farm Stays in Spain

Consider booking a room in a traditional Basque farmhouse (caserío or etxe) for a genuinely local experience. Here, you can enjoy genuine hospitality, regional food, and farm life.

- Zelai-Eder Agrotourism (San Sebastián, Spain)

    - Ideal for: Culinary enthusiasts and cultural adventurers
    - Why stay? This family-owned farmhouse provides culinary lessons, farm-to-table meals, and a genuine rural experience.
    - Highlights: Interactive farm experiences, homemade Basque cheese and cider, and stunning rural vistas.
- Ferme Landran (County of the French Basques)

    - Ideal for: Travelers looking for a leisurely, genuine experience
    - Why stay? Enjoy home-cooked meals, learn about regional agriculture, and unwind in the

tranquil countryside at this working Basque farm.

○ Highlights: Goat cheese production, verdant pastures, and easy access to beautiful hiking routes.

Guidelines and Advice for Wild Camping

Wild camping is an option for seasoned campers who want a more remote experience, but there are stringent regulations to adhere to in both the French and Spanish Basque areas.

Is It Legal to Camp Wild in the Basque Country?

- Spain (Basque Country & Navarre): Although wild camping is technically prohibited, discreet overnight visits in isolated mountain regions are usually accepted as long as you leave no trace and abide by local laws.
- France (Basque Country & Pyrenees): Campfires are strictly forbidden, but bivouac camping (camping for just one night between sunset and daybreak) is allowed above 1,000 meters in the Pyrenees.

Advice for Conscientious Wild Camping

- Leave No Trace: Remove all garbage, reduce your impact, and show nature respect.
- Camp Away from Roads and Villages: Pick a remote location at least one kilometer away from the closest community.
- Steer Clear of Private Property: If in doubt, always get permission.
- No Open Fires: During dry seasons, use a portable stove to reduce fire risks.
- Show Consideration for Locals and Wildlife: Minimize noise and avoid disturbing nearby farms or animals.

Top Wild Camping Locations (Where Permitted)

- Bivouac camping is permitted in isolated alpine regions of France's Pyrenees National Park.
- Gorbeia Natural Park (Spain): Secluded valleys and forests for peaceful overnight stays.
- Irati Forest (Navarre, Spain): One of the largest beech forests in Europe, offering serene areas and a rich landscape.

The Basque Country provides incredible outdoor experiences, whether you sleep beneath the Pyrenees' peaks, wake up to the Atlantic's roaring waves, or stay in a comfortable treehouse amidst the woods. There are amazing mountain and coastal campsites for those who enjoy roughing it. If you want a little more comfort, rural farmhouses, eco-lodges, and glamping locations provide a distinctive way to take in the breathtaking scenery and vibrant culture of the area.

Make the most of your outdoor experience in the Basque Country by appreciating the beauty of nature, respecting the environment, and staying wherever you choose!

Basque Cuisine & Gastronomic Adventures

An Overview of Basque Food

In the Basque Country, food is more than just food; it's a way of life. Every meal is an opportunity to enjoy centuries-old culinary traditions and the freshest local ingredients, whether you're in the ancient cider houses of the countryside or the busy pintxos bars of San Sebastián.

The region's rocky coastline, lush valleys, and mountain meadows are all reflected in the cuisine of the Basques, which has strong roots in both land and sea. With an emphasis on premium seafood, grass-fed meat, seasonal vegetables, and artisanal cheeses, the flavors are robust but straightforward. Every mouthful reveals a tale of Basque ingenuity and legacy, whether it's a plate of bacalao al pil-pil (salt cod in a garlic emulsion), a flawlessly grilled txuleta (Basque beef), or a simple yet sophisticated pintxo.

One of the must-see places in Europe for foodies is the Basque Country. This place is a haven for both gourmet tourists and informal food enthusiasts, offering both Michelin-starred fine dining and filling traditional meals.

Must-Try Recipes: Txuleta, Pintxos, and More

These classic meals ought to be at the top of your list, whether you're dining at a remote Basque farmhouse for a long, leisurely lunch or hopping between pintxos bars in Bilbao.

1. The Center of Basque Social Life: Pintxos

The Basque counterpart of tapas, pintxos (pronounced "peen-chos") are little, creatively prepared morsels that are offered in taverns all across the region. In the evenings, locals congregate to visit various bars and try various pintxos while sipping on a drink of wine or cider from the area.

- Gilda – A straightforward but tasty skewer of pickled guindilla peppers, green olives, and anchovies.

- Txangurro – A rich and flavorful crab-stuffed shell, frequently found along the coast.
- Foie Gras with Apple Compote – A rich pintxo that combines sweet apple and creamy foie gras.
- Bacalao (Salt Cod) Pintxos – Frequently served with pil-pil sauce, a delectable mixture of olive oil and garlic.

2. The Iconic Basque Steak, Txuleta

Txuleta is the quintessential representation of the world's greatest beef, which can be found in Basque Country. The strong flavor of the grass-fed beef is highlighted by the simple seasoning of sea salt on this enormous, bone-in ribeye steak grilled over an open flame.

- Best places to try it:
  - *Casa Julián (Tolosa)*
  - *Asador Etxebarri (Axpe)*

3. A Basque Classic: Bacalao al Pil-Pil

This dish, which consists of salt cod cooked slowly in olive oil and garlic until it becomes a silky, emulsified sauce, exemplifies the Basque mastery of seafood.

- Best places to try it:

- A restaurant on the sea in Getaria
- The old town of Bilbao

4. The Fisherman's Stew, or Marmitako

Marmitako is a hearty stew of tuna, potatoes, onions, and peppers that is slow-cooked in a flavorful broth, originally served to Basque fishermen.

- Best places to try it:
  - *Traditional beach eateries like Lekeitio or Hondarribia*

5. Idiazabal Cheese: The Basque Mountains' Pride

One of the most well-known culinary exports from the Basque Country, this smoky, somewhat nutty sheep's milk cheese is often grated over food or served with quince paste.

- Best places to try it:
  - *A local market*
  - *A cheese farm in the Basque countryside*

6. The Perfect Dessert: Basque Cheesecake

Basque burnt cheesecake differs from other types of cheesecake in that it has a creamy, custard-like core and a charred top.

- Best place to try it:
  - *La Viña, San Sebastián (the birthplace of the original recipe)*

The Function of Conventional Dining Establishments and Cider Houses

A Rustic Gastronomic Adventure in Basque Cider Houses

A trip to a traditional sagardotegi (cider house) is among the most distinctive eating experiences in the Basque Country. House-made Basque cider is served directly from enormous oak barrels in these rustic venues, which are frequently housed in former farmhouses. With a set menu that focuses on txuleta, salt fish, and regional cheeses, the dining experience is energetic and communal.

Expectations for a Cider House:

- Txotx Ritual – A convivial and enjoyable event where guests congregate around wooden barrels and alternately catch cider in their cups as it pours out.

- Simple, Filling Meals – Common dishes include walnuts with cheese and quince paste, grilled txuleta, and saltfish omelets.
- Best Time to Go – Although many cider houses are open all year round, the cider season runs from January to April.

Where to Go:

- Sidrería Petritegi – Located close to San Sebastián, this well-known cider house offers a genuine experience.
- Sidrería Gartziategi (Astigarraga) – A family-run cider house known for its excellent txuleta.

Classic Basque Dining Establishments: Celebrating Centuries of Superior Cuisine

Some of the greatest restaurants in the world, from Michelin-starred establishments to family-run taverns that have honed their recipes over decades, can be found in the Basque Country for a more formal yet genuine dining experience.

- Asador Etxebarri (Axpe, Spain) – Frequently listed as one of the greatest restaurants in the world, renowned for its wood-fired grilling methods.
- Arzak (San Sebastián, Spain) – A pioneer of modern Basque cuisine, fusing creativity with tradition.
- Casa Urola (San Sebastián, Spain) – Offers traditional seafood dishes with a modern twist.

The Basque Country offers one of the most exquisite gastronomic experiences in Europe, whether you're having a world-class steak, a long, leisurely lunch at a cider house, or a pintxo-drinking spree. Every meal, from the mountains to the sea, narrates a tale of creativity, tradition, and a lifelong love of food. Come hungry, eat well, and experience the mouthwatering flavors of Basque cuisine wherever your journey takes you!

Culinary Travel

Cider and Wine

With its unique combination of world-class wines, traditional cider, and some of the most renowned restaurants on the planet, the Basque Country is a foodie's and drink lover's paradise. This area encourages you to enjoy every moment, whether you're exploring sun-drenched vineyards with a view of the ocean, enjoying a multi-course tasting menu at a Michelin-starred restaurant, or sipping cider directly from the barrel in a rural farmhouse.

Vineyards and Wine Tours in Txakoli

The Txakoli (pronounced "cha-ko-lee") is a must-try if you enjoy crisp, refreshing wines. The pride of the Basque Country, this light, gently effervescent white wine is renowned for its bracing acidity and zesty citrus flavors, making it the ideal accompaniment to shellfish and pintxos.

Three important regions are the main producers of Txakoli:

- Getariako Txakolina (Gipuzkoa Province): The most famous, producing crisp, fresh wines with a hint of natural spritz.
- Bizkaiko Txakolina (Biscay Province): Has a slightly larger body with notes of minerality and apple.
- Arabako Txakolina (Álava Province): The least popular but produces wines that are a little more structured.

Top Vineyards to Visit

1. Txomin Etxaniz (Getaria): One of the most renowned and historic producers of Txakoli, with breathtaking views of the Bay of Biscay.
2. Hiruzta Bodega (Hondarribia): An innovative yet traditional winery offering wonderful guided tours.
3. Doniene Gorrondona (Bakio): Located near Bilbao, this winery uses sustainable and organic methods to make Txakoli.

Wine Tasting Experience

Most wineries provide tastings accompanied by regional specialties, including fresh seafood, Getaria anchovies, and Idiazabal cheese. Understanding Basque culture and the close relationship between the land and its flavors is just as important as tasting the wine on a vineyard visit.

Cider Houses and Tasting Experiences in the Basque Country

In the countryside, sagardoa, or Basque cider, is the preferred beverage. Made from a variety of local apple varieties, Basque cider is dry, acidic, and slightly effervescent, in contrast to the sweeter ciders found elsewhere in the world.

The Experience of the Cider House

A trip to a sagardotegi (cider house) offers a whole cultural experience in addition to cider tasting. Most cider houses have a traditional set menu that includes:

- Salt cod omelet: Eggs and salted fish combined to create a tender, delicious delicacy.
- Grilled txuleta (Basque steak): A beautifully browned, bone-in ribeye cooked over an open flame.
- Walnuts, cheese, and quince paste: A classic cider house dessert combination.

Txotx! The Ritual of Cider

One of the highlights of visiting a cider house is the Txotx! ritual, where the proprietor unlocks a huge wooden cider barrel, and patrons line up to pour the cider straight into their glasses. It is a vibrant, social, and authentically Basque tradition.

The Best Cider Houses to Visit

1. Sidrería Petritegi (Astigarraga): One of the most well-known cider establishments, offering great food and guided tastings.
2. Sidrería Zelaia (Hernani): Renowned for its excellent cider and authentic ambiance.
3. Sidrería Gartziategi (Astigarraga): A lovely, rustic farmhouse setting for this historic cider house.

The best time to visit is during the cider season from January to April, though many cider houses remain open year-round, offering tastings and tours.

Basque Country Dining with **Michelin Stars**

With more Michelin-starred restaurants per person than almost anywhere else on Earth, the Basque Country is often called the gastronomic capital of the world. The Basque love of food is reflected in an elegant dining scene that blends traditional methods with modern creativity.

The Center of Fine Dining in **San Sebastián**

San Sebastián alone boasts multiple Michelin-starred restaurants, making it a must-visit destination for food lovers:

- Arzak (3 Michelin stars): A family-run restaurant known for its innovative New Basque cuisine.
- Akelarre (3 Michelin stars): A restaurant featuring a cutting-edge tasting menu with stunning coastal views.
- Martín Berasategui (3 Michelin stars): The most Michelin-starred chef in Spain offers a flawless fine dining experience.

Beyond **Bilbao**

Bilbao and other parts of the Basque Country also feature exceptional Michelin-starred dining:

- Azurmendi (3 Michelin stars, near Bilbao): A sustainable farm-to-table restaurant using local ingredients.
- Nerua (1 Michelin star, Bilbao): Located inside the Guggenheim Museum, blending art and food in a sleek, modern setting.
- Etxebarri (1 Michelin star, Axpe): A paradise for grilled cuisine, where everything—from butter to fish—is cooked over an open flame.

Tips for Dining at Michelin-Starred Restaurants

- Make reservations well in advance. Many top restaurants book up months ahead, especially during peak travel seasons.
- Consider lunch instead of dinner. Many Michelin-starred restaurants offer more affordable midday tasting menus.
- Balance fine dining with casual pintxos bars. Some of the best tapas experiences happen while sipping a glass of Txakoli in a lively pintxos bar. The Basque culinary scene is about finding harmony between high-end dining and local flavors.

The Basque Country is an unmatched destination for food and wine tourism, offering everything from the bold, rustic appeal of Basque cider to the crisp, sea-kissed flavors of Txakoli wine. Whether you're enjoying a relaxed cider house feast, a sun-drenched wine tour, or a once-in-a-lifetime Michelin-starred meal, every sip and bite is a celebration of tradition, innovation, and a deep love for fine food.

This is more than just a place to visit for authentic Basque cuisine—it's an unforgettable journey through one of the most fascinating culinary traditions on Earth.

Examining Basque Towns and Cities

In the Basque Country, modernity, culture, and history coexist harmoniously to create cities and towns that are as dynamic as they are varied. Every place has a unique personality that makes it enjoyable to explore, from the world-famous food and golden beaches of San Sebastián to the avant-garde art scene of Bilbao and the French Basque charm of Biarritz and Bayonne.

San Sebastián: Cuisine, Culture, and Beaches

The gem in the crown of Basque cities is San Sebastián, also known as Donostia in Basque, where the intensity of a thriving culinary scene blends with the rhythm of the waves. It is a haven for tourists who enjoy gourmet eating, outdoor exploration, and cultural discovery because of its breathtaking coastline, Belle Époque architecture, and Michelin-starred restaurants.

San Sebastián's Best Experiences

- Unwind on the beach at La Concha
  One of the world's most exquisite urban
  beaches is this crescent-shaped bay. It's
  the ideal place for a leisurely day
  because of its beautiful promenade,
  clean waters, and soft golden sand. Visit
  Zurriola Beach, a favorite among
  surfers, or Ondarreta Beach for more
  privacy.

- Savor the Scene of Pintxos
  San Sebastián is well-known for its
  pintxos, which are tiny, upscale snacks
  offered in pubs all across the Old Town
  (Parte Vieja).

  Must-see bars:

  - For the renowned Txuleta steak,
    visit Bar Néstor.
  - San Telmo's Cuchara
    (contemporary Basque pintxos).
  - Gandarias (traditional pintxos of
    Iberian ham and shellfish).
- Scale Monte Igueldo for sweeping vistas
  To see the stunning coastline of San
  Sebastián, ride the funicular up Monte

Igueldo.

- Explore the Old Town's Historic District
  Explore the quaint streets, including stops at Plaza de la Constitución, a former bullring, and San Vicente Church.

- Go to the Museum of San Telmo
  This museum, housed in a magnificently renovated 16th-century monastery, is a must-see for history buffs. It features Basque art, culture, and tradition.

From the Guggenheim to Old Town in Bilbao

Bilbao is a city undergoing change, with its industrial foundations giving way to a flourishing center of culture and cuisine. While the Nervión River meanders through its bustling streets, sleek new architecture coexists with historic structures.

Best Things to Do in Bilbao

- Take in the Guggenheim Museum with wonder
  This well-known museum was created

by Frank Gehry and is a masterwork of architecture. It is a must-see because of the titanium curves, Jeff Koons' "Puppy" sculpture, and the modern art exhibits.

- Tour the Old Town, or Casco Viejo
  Bilbao's medieval center is teeming with lively bars, colorful architecture, and winding streets.

  - See the oldest structure in the city, Santiago Cathedral.
  - Visit local hotspots like Gure Toki and Café Iruña to sample traditional pintxos and Basque cider.

- Take a stroll via La Ribera Market and the Nervión River
  A beautiful walk along the restored riverbank is highly recommended. Visit La Ribera Market, a sizable indoor food market where you may sample local specialties, fresh meats, and seafood.

- Go across the bridge in Zubizuri
  Santiago Calatrava's futuristic white footbridge provides breathtaking views of Bilbao's changing skyline.

- Take Artxanda by Funicular
  Hiking trails and a tranquil haven from the bustle of the city may be found atop the Artxanda Funicular, which offers the best panoramic views of Bilbao.

Bayonne & Biarritz: French Basque Charm

Biarritz: The Elegance of the Sea and Surfing

Biarritz is a glamorous and adventurous coastal city that combines French elegance with Basque culture. Once a favorite retreat of European royalty, it is now a stunning seaside town and a surfers' paradise.

The Best Activities in Biarritz

- Go to the Grand Plage and hit the waves
  The Grand Plage is a great spot to surf or just take in the scenery in Biarritz, one of Europe's best surfing locations.

- Visit Rocher de la Vierge
  Unmatched views of the shoreline may be seen from this striking rock formation, which includes a statue of the Virgin Mary.

- Examine the Market in the Halles de Biarritz
Fresh produce, fish, cheeses, and Basque specialties abound in this bustling market, which is ideal for a picnic or a quick snack.

- Step into the Hôtel du Palais
This famous five-star hotel, which was first constructed for Empress Eugénie, offers a window into Biarritz's aristocratic history.

A Snip of Real Basque Culture in Bayonne

Just inland from Biarritz, Bayonne is a more sedate but incredibly genuine place that is well-known for its half-timbered homes, fascinating history, and mouthwatering cuisine.

The Best Activities in Bayonne

- Take a stroll through charming Old Town
Stroll down the Nive River, where the waterfront is lined with quaint Basque

homes with vibrant shutters.

- ○ Discover the UNESCO World Heritage Site, the Gothic-style Bayonne Cathedral.
- Sample the well-known chocolate from Bayonne
  Since the 17th century, Bayonne has been known for producing chocolate. To get a sense of the past, visit a chocolatier such as Cazenave.

- Go to the Museum of Basque Art
  Set in a 17th-century mansion, it offers an excellent introduction to Basque customs, history, and language.

- Sample real Bayonne ham
  One of the most well-known treats in the area is jambon de Bayonne, which is aged for months and has the ideal balance of flavor and salt.

From the golden beaches of San Sebastián to Bilbao's contemporary resurgence to the French Basque charm of Biarritz and Bayonne, each city and town in the Basque Country has a unique narrative to tell. The Basque spirit of adventure and tradition permeates every aspect of life, whether you're touring medieval old towns, surfing world-class waves, or dining at Michelin-starred restaurants.

You will be captivated by the vitality, natural beauty, and rich cultural heritage that make the Basque Country one of the world's most remarkable travel destinations, regardless of where your adventure starts.

Traditions, History, and Culture of the Basques

Deeply ingrained customs, lively festivals, and a cultural identity that has endured over time may all be found in the Basque Country. In contrast to other parts of Europe, the Basques have managed to maintain their rich folklore, music, and dance, their unique sports, and their old language, Euskara, all of which are still very much alive today. You'll soon discover that the Basque spirit is still very much alive and well, whether you're exploring old towns, watching a fierce game of pelota, or taking in the heartfelt sounds of traditional txalaparta music.

Euskara: The Basques' Ancient Language

The Euskara language is one of the most intriguing facets of Basque identity. One of the oldest and most enigmatic languages in the world, Euskara has no known linguistic relations, unlike Spanish or French. Although its origins are still up for question, it is a linguistic treasure because it existed before Indo-European languages arrived in the area.

A Survival Language

Euskara persevered in the face of centuries of outside influence, including Roman domination and the monarchs of Spain and France. The language was restricted and outlawed in schools and public life during the 20th century, especially in Spain during Franco's dictatorship. But following Franco's reign, a cultural renaissance gave rise to the resurrection of Euskara, which is now an official language of Spain's Basque Country, alongside Spanish. Euskara is still being preserved and promoted in France, and ikastolak, or Basque language schools, are an important part of this effort.

Acquiring a Few Words

Although many people speak French and Spanish, locals value tourists who try to communicate using Euskara. Here are some helpful expressions:

- Kaixo – Hi
- Eskerrik Asko – I'm grateful
- Agur – Farewell
- Ongi etorri – Welcome

- Zenbat da? – What is the cost?

Euskara is frequently the main language in smaller communities, and hearing it spoken well serves as a reminder of the area's distinct identity.

Conventional Sports: Rowing and Pelota Contests

Sports, but not just any sports, are very important to the Basques. Entire communities gather here to observe, participate, and celebrate traditional games that have been a part of the local culture for decades.

The Quick-Paced Wall Sport: Pelota

One of the most recognizable Basque sports is pelota, also known as pelota vasca, which is played on frontón courts that can be found in almost every town and hamlet. Played with bare hands, paddles, or baskets (cesta punta), it's a fast-paced ball game that's frequently likened to squash.

- Known as "the fastest ball game in the world," jai alai is the most well-known form, with balls traveling at nearly 300 km/h (186 mph).

- Pelota battles are fierce, with competitors showcasing amazing power, speed, and accuracy.
- You'll probably see a live match if you go during a local festival, where fervent supporters will be cheering for the players from their hometown.

Rowing Contests: A Tradition of Seafaring

The Basque Country's rowing events, known as traineras, highlight its close ties to the water. Fishing customs gave rise to these races, in which teams would row longboats out to sea and return, vying for the first catch. Rowers now practice all year long for competitive regattas that are conducted along the coast, attracting sizable crowds and tough competition.

- Teams row on the breathtaking La Concha Bay during the Bandera de la Concha, one of the most important events, which takes place in San Sebastián every September.
- Thousands of people line the shore, cheering their teams on, and the energy is electric.

Dance, Music, and Folklore: An Ongoing Tradition

Traditional music and dance are performed at festivals, family get-togethers, and even on the streets of ancient towns, demonstrating how deeply ingrained Basque folklore is in everyday life.

The Essence of Basque Festivities: Music

The unusual melodies and rhythmic beats of traditional Basque music can evoke strong emotions. Among the most distinctive instruments are:

- Txalaparta – Two musicians play this wooden percussion instrument in a rhythmic back-and-forth fashion. Originally employed as a means of communication among farmhouses, it is today an essential component of Basque music.
- Trikitixa – The Basque diatonic accordion that adds vibrant energy to celebrations and parties.
- Alboka – A distinctive wind instrument from Spain, often heard in folk music performances, played continuously like a bagpipe.

A thriving Basque folk-rock movement has emerged in recent years as a result of the blending of traditional and new sounds. Bands such as Kortatu, Negu Gorriak, and Kalakan have achieved international acclaim.

A Sign of Basque Pride: Dancing

Basque dancing is a storytelling heritage rather than only a show. Each stride, motion, and arrangement reflects ideas of joy, strength, and community and has historical and cultural value.

Among the most well-known traditional dances are:

- Aurresku – A beautiful and very significant dance that is frequently done at formal ceremonies, weddings, and other special occasions. It shows a lone dancer clutching a hat while performing complex footwork.
- Jota and Fandango – Vivacious partner dances that are frequently performed during local festivals to live trikitixa music.
- Mutildantza – A group circle dance in which dancers move in sync to represent tradition and togetherness.

In the Basque Country, people dance in town squares, especially during summer festivals, and invite guests to join in the fun.

Basque Identity Preservation and Celebration

Basque culture is living, active, and being proudly carried into the future; it is not a thing of the past. The Basques have maintained their language, customs, and sports in spite of historical obstacles, guaranteeing that their identity is robust and alive.

For tourists, immersing themselves in Basque culture involves more than merely watching—it is about getting involved. You join this rich and long tradition whether you're:

- Applauding at a pelota game
- Sampling cider in a traditional sagardotegi
- Picking up a few words of Euskara
- Dancing in the streets during a festival

When you visit the Basque Country, take the time to listen, see, and experience the local way of life. You will come away from your trip with more than just memories—you will gain a profound respect for people who have embraced modernity while clinging to their traditions.

12. Events & Festivals in 2025

The Basque Country is home to colorful customs, fervent festivals, and celebrations that spectacularly unite local communities. Every event in 2025 promises to be a remarkable experience, whether it's the exhilarating intensity of Pamplona's Running of the Bulls, the deafening drumbeats of La Tamborrada, or the culinary delights of food festivals that highlight the area's well-known pintxos and cider. You may experience the Basque way of life, which is full of excitement, tradition, and cultural pride, up close if you schedule your trip to the Basque Country during one of these renowned festivals.

The Legendary Festival of The Running of the Bulls (San Fermín) in Pamplona

San Fermín, one of the most well-known events worldwide, turns Pamplona into a thrilling display of tradition and excitement. Thousands of people celebrate in traditional Basque and Navarrese fashion every year from July 6th to July 14th, flooding the streets in traditional white attire and red scarves.

Bull Run's Heart-Pounding Encierro

The most famous San Fermín event is the Encierro, or Running of the Bulls, in which twelve strong bulls chase fearless (or careless) runners as they dash through Pamplona's winding streets. The community holds its breath as competitors sprint through an 875-meter (half-mile) route every morning at 8 AM, culminating in the historic bullring.

- Top Viewing Locations: Locals reserve these popular locations in advance, so the ideal site to observe is from a balcony with a view of the streets. If not, arrive early in the Plaza Consistorial to guarantee a spot along the path.
- Becoming a Runner: This is not for the faint of heart! To participate, you must be at least eighteen, sober, and physically fit.
- The Festive Spirit: With parades, pyrotechnics, live music, and countless celebrations that go on deep into the night, the atmosphere is electrifying even if you don't run.

Beyond just the bull run, San Fermín is a week-long burst of Basque culture that combines tradition, history, and pure excitement.

La Tamborrada: San Sebastián's Thunderous Drum Festival

A unique acoustic display awaits you if you visit San Sebastián on January 20th. At the 24-hour drumming celebration known as La Tamborrada, thousands of drummers march through the streets, bringing the entire city to life with their unrelenting rhythm.

A Celebration of Harmony and Sound

- The city's flag is raised by the mayor of San Sebastián at the Plaza de la Constitución at the stroke of midnight, marking the beginning of continuous drumming performances.
- The air is filled with booming rhythms as hundreds of marching bands pass through the streets, clad in classic military costumes or chef's attire.
- Both locals and tourists participate in the celebration, dancing, clapping, and honoring San Sebastián's rich past.
- The city is silent once more, marking the conclusion of the festival—until the next year—exactly twenty-four hours later.

La Tamborrada is a unique opportunity to witness Basque tradition at its most raucous and intense if you enjoy music, culture, and exuberant festivities.

The Largest Celebration in the Basque Country: Semana Grande

Every August, the cities of San Sebastián, Bilbao, and Vitoria-Gasteiz celebrate Semana Grande (Aste Nagusia), a week-long summer celebration packed with street entertainment, music, and fireworks.

Fireworks and Celebrations

- Fireworks Competitions: Over La Concha Bay in San Sebastián or along the Nervión River in Bilbao, a different pyrotechnic team lights up the sky every night in a stunning display.
- Giant Puppets (Gigantes y Cabezudos): Tall papier-mâché figurines enchant both adults and children as they dance around the streets.
- Live Dance and Music: Stages appear all throughout the city, showcasing international acts, contemporary rock bands, and traditional Basque music.

- Opening Ceremony (Txupinazo): The event begins with a rocket launch, marking the start of a week of nonstop festivities.

Semana Grande is the place to go if you want to experience the largest summer fiesta in the Basque Country.

Culinary Events and Food Festivals: A Feast for the Senses

A food lover's dream, the Basque Country hosts numerous culinary festivals all year long to honor its renowned cuisine. These festivals ought to be on your 2025 travel itinerary if you have a strong interest in Michelin-starred restaurants, fresh seafood, Basque cider, or pintxos.

Pintxos Contests: Savor the Finest Basque Food

- A staple of Basque cuisine, pintxos (tiny, savory morsels eaten on bread) are the subject of annual competitions in cities such as San Sebastián, Bilbao, and Vitoria-Gasteiz to determine the finest chef.

- Experience these events in April or September, when chefs use local ingredients to create inventive and delectable pintxos.
- Explore the Old Towns, where pubs vie to offer the tastiest and most inventive food.
- Take part in a pintxos crawl and try everything from contemporary haute cuisine inventions to the classic gilda (anchovy, olive, and pepper skewers).

Sagardo Apurua: The Basque Cider Festival

Visitors can sample freshly brewed Basque cider direct from the barrel at this November festival in San Sebastián, which brings traditional cider houses (sagardotegis) into the city.

- Enjoy your cider with regional cheeses, salt fish omelets, and grilled txuleta (Basque steak).
- See how cider is traditionally poured in the Basque Country, where it is poured from a height to aerate it before consumption.
- Discover the warmth of the Basques as they invite guests to partake in their cider-drinking customs.

Getaria's Seafood Festival

Getaria, a seaside town, celebrates its renowned grilled fish (parrillada de pescado) with a seafood festival in May. It is one of the greatest spots to sample freshly caught tuna, hake, and anchovies that have been properly prepared over open flames.

- As eateries along the waterfront serve their specialties, take in the aroma of fresh fish cooking outdoors.
- Try the crisp white wine from the area, Txakoli, which pairs perfectly with seafood.
- Watch competitions and cooking demos that highlight Basque grilling methods.

One place that knows how to celebrate is the Basque Country. 2025 is looking to be a year filled with unforgettable events, whether you're viewing fireworks above Bilbao, dancing to the thunder of San Sebastián's drums, seeking adrenaline in Pamplona, or indulging in top-notch cuisine.

If you schedule your vacation around these occasions, you will not only experience Basque culture but also become a part of it.

Basque Is Family-Friendly

Families will love the Basque Country because it provides the ideal balance of outdoor activities, kid-friendly dining, and fascinating cultural experiences. The Basque Country offers something for everyone, whether your family enjoys hands-on history learning, culinary exploration, or environmental discovery. This area is the perfect playground for inquisitive minds and energetic young explorers, offering everything from entertaining beaches and accessible hiking paths to interactive museums and traditional festivals.

This guide will assist you in finding the top attractions, restaurants, and cultural events in the Basque Country for your family's trip, guaranteeing a memorable time for both children and adults.

The Greatest Outdoor Activities for Children

Days at the Beach in the Bay of Biscay

There are many lovely, kid-friendly beaches along the Basque coast where children may play in the water safely, make sandcastles, and splash in the gentle waves.

- La Concha Beach (San Sebastián) – One of Spain's most well-known urban beaches, La Concha is ideal for families due to its gentle sand, serene waters, and abundance of ice cream shops nearby.
- Hondarribia Beach – Close to the French border, this beach is popular with young children and features grassy picnic areas, a playground, and shallow waters.
- Grand Plage (Biarritz) – If your family is interested in surfing, this beach provides kid-friendly lessons so they can learn how to ride the waves in a fun and safe environment.

Easy Hikes and Beautiful Walks

With short, picturesque routes that are appropriate for children of all ages, the Basque Country is a fantastic place for family hikes due to its breathtaking scenery.

- The Flysch Route (Zumaia) – This short coastal walk is a great way to spark children's interest in geology and ecology as it passes by cliffs dotted with fossils and striking rock formations.
- Bosque Pintado (Painted Forest of Oma) – Brightly painted trees make for an engaging and colorful hiking experience that children will love.
- Monte Igueldo Funicular & Viewpoint (San Sebastián) – Ride a historic funicular to the summit for breathtaking panoramic views and a small amusement park with old carnival rides.

Nature Parks and Animal Interactions

The Basque Country offers a number of engaging experiences for children who are passionate about animals and wildlife.

- Txiki Park (Bilbao) – A nature adventure park designed for young explorers, featuring zip lines, climbing walls, and treetop rope courses.
- Donostia Aquarium (San Sebastián) – One of Spain's best aquariums, where children can explore an underwater tunnel surrounded by vibrant fish and sharks.

- Euskal Herria Animal Park (Sara, France) – A wonderful place where children can visit and feed local animals such as Basque horses, sheep, and goats.

Family-Friendly Dining Options & Cuisine

Kid-Friendly Basque Recipes

Fortunately, many of the Basque Country's famous dishes are kid-friendly. The region is renowned for its exceptional cuisine.

- Pintxos for All Ages – While some pintxos are adventurous, many bars serve simple yet delicious options like croquettes (*croquetas*), Spanish omelets (*tortilla de patatas*), and ham and cheese sandwiches (*bocadillos*).
- Basque Steak (*Txuleta*) – A succulent grilled steak, often served with crispy fries—ideal for children who love meat!
- Basque Cheesecake (*Tarta de Queso*) – A rich, caramelized cheesecake that makes the perfect family dessert.

Top Family-Friendly Dining Establishments

- Casa Gandarias (San Sebastián) – A well-known pintxos bar featuring kid-friendly selections and a warm atmosphere.

- El Globo (Bilbao) – A great choice for families, offering delicious small plates that children can sample at their own pace.
- Zazpi (Vitoria-Gasteiz) – A laid-back restaurant serving regional cuisine with plenty of options for young eaters.

For families who want a more hands-on culinary experience, attending a cider house (*sagardotegi*) or enrolling in a cooking class can be a fun and delicious way to learn about Basque cuisine.

Engaging Cultural Experiences

Interactive Museums and Exhibits

The Basque Country has a variety of museums and cultural institutions designed to entertain children with interactive displays.

- Eureka! Science Museum (San Sebastián) – A fantastic place where children can learn about physics, robotics, and space through hands-on experiments.

- Maritime Museum (Bilbao) – An engaging museum where young adventurers can learn about the region's seafaring history, climb aboard historic boats, and try out sailing simulators.
- Baiona Chocolate Museum (France) – A museum dedicated to the history of chocolate in the Basque Country, offering kid-friendly chocolate-making classes and tastings.

Holidays & Customs for Families

Attending a festival is a wonderful way for families to experience Basque music, dance, and traditions.

- Parades and Giant Puppets (Semana Grande, August) – *Gigantes y Cabezudos*, enormous puppet figures, parade through the streets in colorful processions.
- San Sebastián Day (La Tamborrada, January 20th) – Children will love watching (and even participating in!) the drumming parades that take over the city for an entire day.
- Basque Rural Sports Championships – Many towns host events featuring traditional Basque sports such as

log-cutting, stone-lifting, and ox-cart pulling, offering a fascinating look into local traditions.

The Benefits of the Basque Country for Families

With its breathtaking scenery, kid-friendly beaches, engaging museums, and mouthwatering cuisine, the Basque Country provides families with an unforgettable travel experience. Whether your children enjoy exploring the outdoors, trying new foods, or engaging in hands-on historical activities, this region offers something for everyone.

By planning your trip around family-friendly locations, exciting activities, and immersive cultural experiences, you can make the most of your time in the Basque Country and create lifelong memories.

Eco-Friendly Travel

The Basque Country is a popular destination for tourists who value the environment, culture, and genuine local experiences because of its wild beaches, verdant mountains, and long-standing customs. Traveling sustainably and responsibly is more crucial than ever as the area gains prominence. Future generations will be able to enjoy this breathtaking region if you travel with eco-consciousness and respect for the environment and people, whether you're trekking the Pyrenees, enjoying regional pintxos, or camping along the rocky coast.

With advice on eco-friendly outdoor activities, ethical tourism, and low-impact camping and hiking, this chapter examines how to reduce your negative effects on the environment while increasing your beneficial contributions to nearby communities.

Eco-Friendly Outdoor Travel and Adventure

Selecting Outdoor Activities That Are Sustainable

The Basque Country is a popular destination for outdoor enthusiasts due to its world-class surfing, beautiful bike routes, and hiking paths. However, maintaining the area's natural beauty depends on selecting eco-friendly activities.

- Hiking and Trail Responsibilities: To avoid erosion and save local vegetation, stay on designated paths in places like Zumaia's Flysch Route or Urkiola Natural Park.
- Respect for Wildlife: Whether you're trekking in the Pyrenees or birdwatching in the Urdaibai Biosphere Reserve, keep an eye on wildlife and never feed them.
- Non-Motorized Water Sports: To lessen pollution in coastal waters and estuaries, choose sailing, paddleboarding, or kayaking over fuel-powered vessels.
- Sustainable Surfing: Many surf schools in Biarritz and San Sebastián provide environmentally friendly programs that involve beach clean-ups and the use of sustainable boards.

How to Lessen Your Carbon Footprint Using Green Transportation

The Basque Country's first-rate public transportation system and bike-friendly communities make it feasible to explore without a car.

- Trains and Buses: Local buses link rural areas with hiking and surfing locations, while the Euskotren and Renfe networks facilitate transit between towns.
- Bicycle-Friendly Paths: Numerous bike lanes may be found in cities like San Sebastián, Bilbao, and Vitoria-Gasteiz, and scenic riding routes along the Basque Coast and Greenways provide an eco-friendly means of transportation.
- Walking-Friendly Cities: From the Old Town of Bilbao to the cliffside walkways of Getaria, many Basque cities are best visited on foot.

Promoting Ethical Travel and Local Businesses

Sustainable Dining: Zero-Waste and Farm-to-Table Establishments

Selecting eateries that use seasonal, locally sourced ingredients is one of the best ways to reduce your carbon footprint and boost the local economy.

- Farmers' Markets: To taste fresh fish, organic produce, and artisan cheeses straight from the source, visit the Ribera Market in Bilbao or La Bretxa Market in San Sebastián.
- Slow Food Restaurants: Using traditional methods and regional ingredients, many Basque restaurants adhere to the slow food philosophy. Seek out eateries that are certified by Euskadi Gastronomika and place a high value on sustainability.
- Pintxos Bars That Produce No Waste: Some pintxos bars, such as San Sebastián's Garbola, have committed to buying from nearby farms, reducing food waste, and utilizing reusable dishes.

Staying in Eco-Friendly Lodging

From energy-efficient downtown hotels to eco-lodges in the mountains, the Basque Country is home to an increasing range of sustainable lodging options.

- Eco-Lodges & Rural Stays: Bermeo's Lurdeia guest house serves organic meals, supports wildlife conservation, and is powered by renewable energy.
- Sustainable City Hotels: Some city hotels, including Barceló Bilbao Nervión, have obtained sustainability certificates for their waste reduction initiatives, water-saving technologies, and solar panel usage.
- Farm Stays (Agroturismos): At family-run agroturismos, visitors can take part in sustainable farming methods, cheese-making, and cider production while experiencing Basque country living and helping out local farmers.

Buying Conscientiously: Handmade Items & Fair Trade Products

To help craftsmen and lessen the environmental impact of imported goods, choose locally crafted crafts and traditional Basque items over mass-produced souvenirs.

- Basque Textiles & Wool Products: Purchase traditional espadrilles, wool blankets, and handmade Basque berets (boinas) by visiting workshops in places like Tolosa or Oñati.

- Ethical Culinary Souvenirs: Select locally produced Idiazabal cheese, organic olive oil, or fair-trade coffee from the Basque Pyrenees.
- Handcrafted Wooden & Ceramic Goods: Beautiful, sustainably sourced hardwood bowls, pottery, and hand-carved furniture are produced by numerous craftspeople in Gernika and Vitoria-Gasteiz.

Low-Impact Hiking and Camping

In order to preserve these beautiful settings, it is imperative that visitors adhere to the Leave No Trace philosophy when camping in the Basque Country.

Selecting Eco-Friendly Campsites

- Certified Eco-Campsites: A few campgrounds, such as Camping Igueldo next to San Sebastián, are certified eco-friendly because they use stringent waste management procedures and renewable energy.
- Respecting Protected Areas: Do not camp in nature reserves or national

parks without the required authorization. Select camping locations that are meant to minimize environmental disturbance instead.

Guidelines and Best Practices for Wild Camping

In the Basque Country, wild camping is strictly prohibited; nonetheless, if it is permitted in some places, abide by these important rules:

- Camp Only in Permitted Zones: Certain areas, particularly those in the Pyrenees and Navarre, permit wild camping with prior permission.
- Pack Out All Trash: Leave your campsite cleaner than when you arrived. Remove all rubbish, including food scraps, to avoid upsetting the local fauna.
- Avoid Open Fires: Because of the risk of wildfire, open fires are frequently forbidden. For cooking, use camping stoves.
- Respect Wildlife and Quiet Hours: Don't damage natural habitats and make as little noise as possible.

Tips for Eco-Friendly Hiking

- Use Reusable Water Bottles: Tap water is safe to drink in most Basque cities, so bring a reusable bottle instead of purchasing plastic ones.
- Follow Designated Trails: In places like Gorbeia Natural Park or the Basque Coastal Trail, stay on marked trails to prevent trampling on nature.
- Carpool or Take Public Transportation to Trailheads: By using a bus or train rather than a car to go to hiking locations, you can cut down on carbon emissions.

In addition to safeguarding the environment, sustainable travel in the Basque Country involves honoring local people, maintaining cultural customs, and making thoughtful travel decisions. You can contribute to ensuring that the Basque Country continues to be a prosperous, stunning, and culturally rich travel destination for many years to come by selecting eco-friendly outdoor activities, patronizing small businesses, and engaging in responsible tourism. You can have a positive experience in the Basque Country—on the land, the people, and your personal travel memories.

Sample Itineraries

Whether you want to walk through untamed mountains, surf world-class waves, savor Michelin-starred food, or discover historic villages with a rich cultural heritage, the Basque Country is a destination that caters to all kinds of travelers. The ideal itinerary is created based on your travel preferences, time constraints, and interests.

We have created three comprehensive itineraries that are suited to various experiences in order to help you get the most out of your trip:

- An exciting 5-day adventure schedule full of outdoor activities.
- A seven-day wine and food trip that highlights the best of Basque cuisine.
- A 10-day highlights program for a comprehensive tour of the French and Spanish Basques.

You can anticipate amazing scenery, friendly service, and life-changing experiences regardless of the route you select.

5-Day Outdoor and Adventure Schedule

Ideal for: Adventurers who wish to actively explore the natural splendor of the Basque Country, such as hikers, surfers, and thrill-seekers.

Day 1: Get to San Sebastián and Go on a Coastal Trek

San Sebastián, the ideal starting point for your journey, is the entry point to both the mountains and the ocean.

- Trek the Camino del Norte coastal trail to Pasaia, a picturesque hike that offers views of rocky bays, cliffs, and verdant surroundings.
- At Pasaia's famous waterfront restaurant, Casa Cámara, savor fresh fish.

Day 2: Exploring Bayonne and Surfing in Biarritz

- Enter the French Basque Country and surf in Biarritz, one of the best places to surf in Europe.
- Take an afternoon trip to Bayonne, which is renowned for its rich chocolate-making heritage,

half-timbered homes, and quaint old
town.
- Spend the night in St. Jean-de-Luz,
which is close to Biarritz.

Day 3: Exploring the Pyrenees by Hiking

- Visit the fabled Pyrenean peak known as
La Rhune. For sweeping vistas, hike or
ride the antique rack railway to the peak.
- Go to Espelette, which is well-known for
its typical Basque farmhouses and red
chili peppers.
- Spend the night back in San Sebastián.

Day 4: Basque Mountains Rock Climbing and
Caving

- Travel to Aizkorri-Aratz Natural Park, a
popular location for rock climbing.
- Discover the ancient geological
structures of Arrikrutz Cave, which is
open to guided excursions for an
underground adventure.
- Spend the night in the natural setting of
Vitoria-Gasteiz.

Day 5: Riding a Bike and Leaving

- The Vitoria Green Ring is an environmentally friendly track that circles the city; rent a bike and ride it.
- Have a last lunch of pintxos and local cider before departing.

7-Day Tour of Food and Wine

Ideal for: Culinary tourists who want to fully experience Basque wine culture, gastronomy, and traditional cuisine.

Day 1: Michelin Stars & Pintxos in San Sebastián

- In the Old Town, check into a boutique hotel.
- Take a pintxos tour that includes traditional foods like jamón ibérico, txangurro (crab), and gilda skewers.
- Savor dinner at the Michelin-starred Arzak or Akelarre restaurants.

Day 2: Coastal Drive & Cider House Experience

- Explore Astigarraga, the Basque Country's cider capital. Savor a classic sidrería dinner while sipping cider from enormous barrels.

- Take a drive down the Basque Coast, with stops at Getaria for wine tastings and grilled seafood.

Day 3: Bilbao: Fine Dining & Market Visit

- Discover the fresh local produce in Europe's largest indoor market, La Ribera Market.
- Attend a guided wine and cheese tasting in the Basque country.
- Eat at the Guggenheim Museum's Michelin-starred restaurant, Nerua.

Day 4: Wine Country of Rioja Alavesa

- Visit Rioja Alavesa, which is home to some of Spain's finest wineries, for a day.
- Take a wine tasting and tour at Marqués de Riscal.
- Before traveling to Vitoria-Gasteiz, have a leisurely lunch at a restaurant with a vineyard view.

Day 5: French Basque Delights in Biarritz and Bayonne

- Visit a traditional chocolatier and explore Bayonne, the cradle of Basque chocolate.

- Have a wine tasting at Saint-Jean-Pied-de-Port after enjoying a seafood meal in Biarritz.

Day 6: Cooking Class and Market Day

- Visit one of the best markets in the area, Tolosa Market, in the morning.
- Take a cooking class in Basque cuisine and learn how to prepare traditional dishes like bacalao al pil-pil.

Day 7: Last Pintxos Crawl and Exit

- Enjoy your final day in San Sebastián by going back to your favorite pintxos bars or purchasing gourmet trinkets from the area.

Highlights of the 10-Day Basque Country Itinerary

Ideal for: Tourists seeking to balance culture, cuisine, history, and nature while seeing the best of both the Spanish and French Basque areas.

Days 1–3: Coastal Villages & San Sebastián

- Day 1: Take a pintxos crawl, walk to Monte Igueldo, and explore La Concha Beach.
- Day 2: Try grilled seafood and tour Getaria, the birthplace of fashion designer Balenciaga.
- Day 3: Explore the Flysch Cliffs in Zumaia, one of Europe's most breathtaking geological formations.

Days 4–5: Bilbao and the Environment

- Day 4: Take a stroll beside the Nervión River and tour the Guggenheim Museum.
- Day 5: Visit Gaztelugatxe, the breathtaking islet made famous by *Game of Thrones*, for the day.

Days 6-7: Basque Towns in France

- Day 6: Take in the stunning beaches of Biarritz.
- Day 7: Take in Bayonne's markets, architecture, and chocolate history.

Days 8–10: Wine Country & the Basque Mountains

- Day 8: Pyrenean hike, with the possibility to stop around La Rhune.
- Day 9: Savor a fine dining experience with wine pairings while touring the vineyards of Rioja Alavesa.
- Day 10: Before leaving, head back to San Sebastián for a leisurely beach day.

Select the Ideal Basque Adventure

The Basque Country has amazing experiences crammed into every schedule, regardless of how much time you have. There is an adventure waiting for you, whether it is ascending the Pyrenees, sampling pintxos bars, or taking in the architecture of the Guggenheim.

Are you prepared to organize your journey? Create your own Basque adventure by combining several destinations and selecting the itinerary that best intrigues you!

Practical Information

Traveling through the Basque Country is a rewarding experience, but having the right practical knowledge can make your trip smoother, safer, and more enjoyable. Whether you're navigating currency exchanges, ensuring your health and safety, or using essential travel apps, being prepared allows you to relax and fully immerse yourself in the region's landscapes, culture, and cuisine.

This section provides key details on currency, safety, emergency contacts, and useful travel resources—everything you need to make your Basque adventure hassle-free.

Currency, Payments, and Tipping

Currency Used in the Basque Country

- Spain (Basque Country): Euro (€)
- France (French Basque Country): Euro (€)

ATMs are widely available, especially in cities like San Sebastián, Bilbao, and Biarritz. Rural areas may have fewer cash machines, so withdraw before heading into remote villages or hiking trails.

Card Payments and Cash

- Credit and debit cards are accepted in most restaurants, shops, and hotels, but smaller pintxos bars, traditional cider houses, and local markets may prefer cash.
- Contactless payments (Apple Pay, Google Pay, etc.) are widely accepted, making transactions quick and easy.
- Always carry some cash for smaller transactions, especially in rural areas or for public transport tickets.

Tipping Culture

Tipping is not obligatory, but rounding up the bill or leaving a small amount is appreciated.

- Restaurants: Round up to the nearest euro or leave 5-10% for exceptional service.
- Bars & Pintxos: Dropping small change in the tip jar is a nice gesture.
- Taxis: Rounding up to the nearest euro is common.

- Hotels: A small tip (€1-2 per bag for porters, €1-3 per day for housekeeping) is appreciated but not expected.

Safety and Health Tips

General Safety

The Basque Country is one of the safest regions in Spain and France, with low crime rates and a welcoming atmosphere. However, basic precautions help ensure a trouble-free trip:

- Pickpocketing: While rare, it can happen in crowded areas like San Sebastián's Old Town, Bilbao's Casco Viejo, or Biarritz's markets. Keep your belongings secure, especially in busy tourist spots.
- Solo Travelers: The Basque Country is safe for solo travelers, including women. Locals are friendly and helpful.
- Hiking & Outdoor Safety: When exploring remote trails, check weather conditions, carry enough water, and download offline maps.

Emergency Numbers

- Spain (Basque Country) Emergency Services: 112 (Police, Fire, Ambulance)

- France (French Basque Country) Emergency Services: 112 (EU-wide emergency number)
- Local Police: Ertzaintza in Spain, Gendarmerie in France (ask locals for the nearest station if needed).

Hospitals

- Bilbao: Hospital Universitario de Basurto (+34 944 006 000)
- San Sebastián: Hospital Donostia (+34 943 007 000)
- Biarritz: Centre Hospitalier de la Côte Basque (+33 5 59 44 35 35)

Healthcare & Travel Insurance

- EU travelers: Bring your European Health Insurance Card (EHIC) for access to public healthcare.
- Non-EU travelers: Travel insurance is highly recommended to cover medical emergencies, trip cancellations, and lost luggage.
- Pharmacies: Easily found in cities and towns, marked by a green cross. Many operate 24/7 on a rotating schedule.

Essential Apps and Resources

Navigation & Transport Apps

- Google Maps – Reliable for walking, public transport, and driving directions.
- Moovit – Best for real-time public transport updates.
- Bizi Biarritz – Bike rental app for cycling in Biarritz and surrounding areas.
- BiziBilbao – Bilbao's public bike-sharing system.
- BlaBlaCar – Popular for carpooling between cities in Spain and France.

Language & Communication

- Google Translate – Useful for translating between Euskara, Spanish, and French.
- Duolingo – Learn basic Spanish, French, or Euskara before your trip.
- SayHi – Real-time voice translation app.

Dining & Local Recommendations

- ElTenedor (TheFork) – Book tables at restaurants, including Michelin-starred spots.

- TripAdvisor – Read reviews of top pintxos bars and restaurants.
- Michelin Guide – Find Basque Country's best fine-dining experiences.

Hiking & Outdoor Apps

- AllTrails – Great for discovering hiking and cycling routes in the Basque mountains and coast.
- Wikiloc – Popular with local hikers for GPS-tracked trails.
- Windy – Provides real-time wind and wave conditions for surfers and water sports lovers.

Money & Currency Conversion

- XE Currency – Check live exchange rates.
- Revolut / Wise – Digital banking apps with low-fee international transactions.

Local Etiquette & Cultural Norms

Greetings & Social Customs

- A kiss on both cheeks is common when greeting friends and family.
- In more formal situations, a handshake is appropriate.

- Locals appreciate polite greetings—say *Kaixo* (hello in Euskara), *Hola* (in Spanish), or *Bonjour* (in French) when entering shops or restaurants.

Dining Etiquette

- Pintxos Bars: Unlike tapas, pintxos are often self-served from the bar. Keep your toothpicks or plates so the bartender can tally your bill.
- Cider Houses: When drinking Basque cider (*sagardoa*), pour from a height to aerate the drink and drink it quickly before it loses its fizz.
- Late Dining: Dinner starts around 8:30-9:30 PM in Spain, while the French side eats earlier (7:00-8:00 PM).

Public Behavior

- Quiet Hours: Many businesses close for siesta (2:00-5:00 PM in Spain), though this is less common in big cities.
- Tipping: Not required but appreciated for great service (see earlier section).
- Beach Norms: In some coastal areas, topless sunbathing is common but not mandatory.

Final Travel Tips for a Smooth Trip

- Always carry a reusable water bottle: Tap water is safe to drink throughout the region.
- Book restaurants in advance: The Basque Country has some of the world's best dining, and reservations fill up quickly.
- Pack layers: Weather can change quickly, especially in the Pyrenees.
- Respect local traditions: The Basque identity is strong, and locals appreciate visitors who show interest in their culture.

By keeping these practical tips in mind, you'll be well-prepared for an amazing journey through the Basque Country, whether you're hiking the Pyrenees, savoring pintxos in San Sebastián, or exploring the charming streets of Biarritz.

Safe travels—*ongi etorri!* (Welcome!)

Made in the USA
Las Vegas, NV
16 March 2025